DOG ROAD WOMAN

POEMS BY ALLISON ADELLE HEDGE COKE

DOG ROAD WOMAN

COFFEE HOUSE PRESS • MINNEAPOLIS

The author wishes to thank the following editors and magazines for publishing work in this book: Lawrence Smith, editor of *Caliban;* Joy Harjo, editor, and Gloria Bird and Beth Cuthand, coeditors of *Reinventing the Enemy's Language;* Leslie Scalapino, editor of *Subliminal Time* from O BOOKS; the editors of *Bombay Gin* 93 and 94; Katie Yates and coeditors of *The Little Magazine;* Jeanette Armstrong, editor of *Looking at the Words of Our People;* the editors of *Exit Zero;* Don Fiddler, editor of *Gatherings IV;* the editors of *It's Not Quiet Anymore* (special thanks to Jon Davis, editing supervisor); the editors of *Voices of Thunder* (special thanks to Arthur Sze, editing supervisor); Jennifer Gray Reddish, editor of *Tribal College Student Magazine; New Poetic Voices of America;* the editors of *the eleventh muse;* and the editors of *13th Moon.*

Coffee House Press is supported in part by a grant provided by the Minnesota State Arts Board, through an appropriation by the Minnesota State Legislature, and by a grant from the National Endowment for the Arts, a federal agency. Additional support has been provided by the Lila Wallace-Reader's Digest Fund; The McKnight Foundation; Lannan Foundation; Jerome Foundation; Target Stores, Dayton's, and Mervyn's by the Dayton Hudson Foundation; General Mills Foundation; The Butler Family Foundation; St. Paul Companies; Honeywell Foundation; Star Tribune/Cowles Media Company; The James R. Thorpe Foundation; Dain Bosworth Foundation; The Beverly J. and John A. Rollwagen Fund of The Minneapolis Foundation; and The Andrew W. Mellon Foundation.

Coffee House Press books are available to the trade through our primary distributor, Consortium Book Sales & Distribution, 1045 Westgate Drive, Saint Paul, MN 55114. For personal orders, catalogs, or other information, write to: Coffee House Press, 27 North Fourth Street, Suite 400, Minneapolis, MN 55401.

Library of Congress CIP Data
Coke, Allison Hedge.
  Dog road woman / Allison A. Hedge Coke.
    p.   cm.
  ISBN 1-56689-061-6 (alk. paper)
    1. Indians of North America—Poetry. 2. Indian women—Poetry.
I. Title
PS3553.04366D64 1997   96-53113
811'.54—DC21   CIP

1 0   9   8   7   6   5   4   3   2   1

Table of Contents

Author Acknowledgments & Dedication

I would like to thank: Lee Ann Brown, Steve Taylor, Peter Lamborn Wilson, and Jeff Grimes for supporting The Year of the Rat as an upcoming chapbook; Anna Lee Walters, editor of *Neon Pow Wow;* Elena Featherston, editor of *Skin Deep: Women Writing on Color, Culture, and Identity;* and all the editors of *Gatherings: The En' owkin Journal of First North American Peoples.*

For assisting this work with awards, residencies, and scholarships, I thank: the New Mexico Press Women's Association for the Doris Gregory Memorial Scholarship Creating Writing Award; the Atlantic Center for the Arts, for an associate residency; the Students for Ethnic Inclusion at Naropa, for the Zora Neale Hurston Scholarship; the Institute of American Indian Arts Creative Writing Department Faculty, for the IAIA Departmental Graduate Creative Writing Award and the Naropa Poetry Prize and scholarship; the Naropa Institute's Creative Writing Department for matching funds for the IAIA Naropa Poetry Prize award and scholarship; and Vermont College for additional support.

For performing with me, I thank: Chris Apache and James Luna. For recording performances, I thank: Lauren Fortmiller for WBAI recording (and Peter Lamborn Wilson for generous air time at the station); Gary Wilson, Diane Reyna, and others at IAIA; Ken Tohe at KUNM; and the Naropa Institute (to SEI and Naropa especially Jack Collom, Anselm Hollo, Anne Waldman, & Katie Yates).

Personal thanks to Milton and Evangeline Apache, Amiri Baraka, Neilwood Begay, Tess Benally, Crystal Bush, Jeff Crews, the Crosses, Jon Davis, Barbara and Bessie Dull Knife, Debra Earling, Linda Fizer, Jessica Hagedorn, Joy Harjo, Lyn Hejinian, Linda Hogan, Angie Kootenhayoo, Loretta Little Hawk, Syd Lea, Garth Lahren (for being a Shoe Gestapo) and Ruth Mustus (for being Stoney Woman), Wilma Mankiller (for her encouragement at Red Clay), Sandy Nakai, Simon J. Ortiz, Ed Sanders, Leslie Scalapino, Maxxine Stevens, Arthur Sze, Char Teeters, Judith Washington, Clay Woody, all the Crawford, Elder, Hyde HedgeCoke, Leatherwood, Shearer, Walker, Watts, Whitaker, Wolf, Gervais, Jarvay, Jarvis, & Enos relations, Walter, my aunties and uncles, and all my loved ones who have traveled on, to the people, to the lands.

This book is dedicated to those who inspired and influenced me, to those who walked with me before and who walk with me still today, and to my sons Travis and Vaughan Hedge Coke.

To Jack and Psa Conroy, Mariah and Allie Weston, Melissa and Shasta Hinkle, Bluebird Mustus Nipshank, Kaene Eagle and Atsatsa Bigknife Antonio for the laughter and the songs.

To Derya Berti, Sandy Hinkle, and Betty Holyan for their endless support, for convincing me to continue with this work and for seeing everything through.

To Charmaine Weston for holding onto the breath of life.

To Janelle Swallow Price, Gino and Molly Bigknife Antonio, Chris Apache, and Ernie Fragua Whitecloud for always being there even when I'm drifting endlessly.

To my parents and sister Stephanie and all my relations.

To some strong-hearted Tsa la gi (Cherokee) people: Grandpa Vaughan, Jim Elk, Carole Marie, Eddie Morrison, and Kim Shuck.

In memory of Bill Ice, Dehl Berti, Bob Weston, Peaches, Escar Vaughan and Maria Louise, Herb and Sybil, Bessie A do he, Susanna Ga na ga, Telitha, Richard, Bernice, Sam, John, Sid, Tom, Willis, and Velma.

TO THE SURVIVORS.

I

The Change

Thirteen years ago,   before bulk barns   and
fifth gear diesel tractors,   we rode royal blue tractors with
toolboxes big enough   to hold a six pack on ice.
In the one hundred fifteen degree   summer
heat   with air   so thick with moisture
you drink as you breathe.
Before the year dusters sprayed
malathion over our clustered bodies,   perspiring
while we primed bottom lugs,
those ground level leaves of tobacco,
and it clung to us with black tar so sticky we rolled
eight-inch balls off our arms at night   and
Cloroxed our clothes for hours and hours.
Before we were poisoned   and
the hospital thought we had been burned in fires,
at least to the third degree,
when the raw, oozing hives that
covered ninety-eight percent of our bodies
from the sprays ordered by the FDA
and spread by   landowners,
before anyone had seen
automated machines that top and prime.
While we topped the lavender
blooms of many tiny flowers
gathered into one,   gorgeous.
By grasping hold below the petals
with our bare, calloused hands
and twisting downward, quick, hard,
only one time,   snapped them off.
Before edgers and herbicides took
what *they*   call weeds,
when we walked for days
through thirty acres   and

chopped them out with hoes.
Hoes,   made long before   from wood and steel
and sometimes (even longer ago)
from wood and deer scapula.
Before the bulk primers came
and we primed all the leaves by hand,
stooped over at the waist for the
lower ones   and   through the season
gradually   rising higher   until   we stood
and worked simultaneously,
as married to the fields as we were to each other,
carrying up to fifty pounds of fresh
leaves under each arm   and   sewing them onto
sticks four feet long on a looper
under the shade of a tin-roofed barn,   made of shingle,
and poking it up through the rafters inside
to be caught by a hanger   who
poked it up higher in the rafters   to another
who held a higher position
and   so   they filled the barn.
And the leaves hung down
like butterfly wings,   though
sometimes the color of
luna moths,   or Carolina parakeets,   when just
an hour ago   they had been
laid upon   the old wooden
cart trailers pulled behind
the orange Allis-Chalmers tractor
with huge, round fenders and only
a screwdriver and salt in the toolbox,
picked by primers   so hot
we would race through the rows
to reach the twenty-five gallon
jugs of water placed throughout
the field to encourage   and   in attempt to
satisfy our insatiable thirsts

from drinking air   which poured
through our pores without breaking
through to our need   for more
water   in the sun.
Sun we imagined to disappear
yet respected   for growing all things on earth
when quenched with rains called forth
by our song   and drumming.
Leaves, which weeks later,   would be
taken down and the strings pulled
like string on top of a large dog-food bag
and sheeted up into burlap sheets
that bundled over a hundred pounds
when we smashed down with our feet,
but gently smashing,
then thrown up high   to
a catcher   on a big clapboard trailer
pulled behind two-ton trucks and
taken to market in Fuquay-Varina
and sold to William Morris   and
Winston-Salem   for around   a buck a pound.
Leaves cured to a bright leaf,
a golden yellow with the strongest
aroma of tobacco barn curing
and hand grown quality
before the encroachment of
big business in the Reagan era
and the slow murder of method
from a hundred years before.
When the loons cried out in
laughter by the springs and
the bass popped the surface on
the pond, early on, next to
the fields, before that time
when it was unfashionable to
transplant each individual baby plant,

the infant tobacco we nurtured, to
transplant those seedlings to each hill
in the field, the space for that particular plant
and we watched   as   they would grow.
Before all of this new age, new way,
I was a sharecropper in Willow Springs, North Carolina,
as were you   and we were proud to be Tsa la gi
wishing for winter   so we could make camp
at Qualla Boundary   and Oconaluftee
would be free of tourists and filled with snow
and those of us who held out forever
and had no CIBs would be home again
with our people, while the BIA forgot to watch.
When we still remembered before even the Europeans,
working now shoulder to shoulder with descendants
of their slaves they brought from Africa
when they sold our ancestors as slaves in the Middle East,
that then the tobacco was sacred to all of us and we
prayed whenever we smoked and
did not smoke for pleasure   and
I   was content and free.
Then they came and changed things
and you left me for a fancy white girl
and I waited on the land
until you brought her back
in that brand new white Trans Am,
purchased from our crop,   you gave her
and left her waiting in a motel.
The nearest one was forty miles away,
but   near enough   for you
and   for her   and I knew   though
I never spoke a word to you
about it,   I knew and I kept it to
myself   to this day   and time   and
I never let on
until I left   on our anniversary.

I drove the pick-up
down the dirt path   by the empty fields
and rented a shack for eighty dollars,
the one with cardboard windows
and a Gillespie house floor design,
with torn and faded floral paper on walls
and linoleum so thin over rotted board
that the floor gave if you weighed over
a hundred pounds.   I did not.
And with no running water of any kind,   or bathroom.
The one at hilltop,   where I could
see out across all the fields
and hunt for meat when I wanted
and find peace.
I heard you remarried
and went into automated farming
and kept up with America.
I watched all of you   from the hill
and I waited for the lavender blooms
to return   and when it was spring
even the blooms   had turned white.
I rolled up my bedroll,   remembering before,
when the fields were like waves on a green ocean,
and turned away,   away from the change
and corruption   of big business on small farms
of traditional agricultural people,   and sharecroppers.
Away,   so that I could always   hold this concise image
of before   that   time   and it
floods   my memory.

Alone Walking

there
has always
been   no one
when
there most
definitely
should   have
been   someone
here   to ease
hardships
endured   thru
this walk
and someone
could   have
definitely
been   there
when
no one
always   was
there

Trace

for Amiri Baraka, Derya, and my sister Stephanie

red hot black stones
beneath thick forest green
army blankets
repelling chill and bite
lying outside
deep inside   blue
light cast on and from ice
blanketing ground in sheets
layered   fourteen times
each   sheet one-inch thick
mirroring   seven point
suns so far away
they look like glitter
and remind us of the dual sun era
when rattlesnake brought back
the daughter sun to the Tsa la gi
seeds   implanted
forever   in the snags of
our minds   carefully folded
into clusters   retaining
their impact and our knowledge
hiding out in our home
the place we held onto
when they tore our people
from its cradle and forced
the walk where
more than three thousand died
where some of us hid even then
and brought back
the sacred heart   of our
emergence place through
a sympathetic white man

one we   took in because he
had ears and heard us and cared
where they made even this
privately owned Indian land
a reservation anyway   and forced
more of us to leave again
in political protest of reservations
and those who stayed to live
as they decided,   some
when venturing out into
the lands that by nature
also are ours   now occupied
by the Americans were even
to be humiliated
to have to use the
color-coded bathrooms
they set up for
the Africans who turned around   breaking
bondage, eliminating constraint, more constraints endured by
the Asians who had left the plains rails,
coming here to this piedmont,
the Latinos who labored
still in migrant campos   and the people
The People   who were
at home here always
even in the 1970s
color-coded bathrooms
white/colored   where
even a blonde-headed girl-child
entered into in public
though she could have   evaded
this humiliation   but refused
to go where some relatives
could not go   because
they were darker complexioned
hiding out in secret

perspectives as old as the
sky above and as
warm as the stones lying
now   beneath her feet
cool, crisp, clean   breaths
inhaled in
tenacious reveling
yellow strands entangled,   mixed,
with the black hair her
sister threw over her
back in lying   to rest   beside   her.

Dog Road Woman

They called you
grandma
Maggie   like
Maggie Valley
I called   on you
for your knowledge
of pieced cotton
I worked clay
to pottery
and thread   to weave
but   had no frame
nor understanding
of pattern
in quilting.
Climbing high
in sacred wood,
which feeds   the
di ni la wi gi   u no do ti,
I captured hickory
twigs   you wanted
for a toothbrush
to dip snuff.
Ninety-two year old
leathered fingers
caressed stitch
and broadcloth
into blanket.
You with your apron
and bonnet
and laughter
at *gold dollars*
and processed meats.
You who taught

me to butcher
without waste
and who spun
stories   on your
card   whenever I
would   listen,
we fashioned stars

Thunder Hawk Meltdown

for Bill T. H.

Pulsating rhythm
like a hoofbeat
on traditional drum.
Off-siding   center
gravitational force,
flinging balance,
unsettling logistics
of perceivable
imagined reality.
Without warning
all preparedness
slips off like
a wave of peels
falling to the floor
in ripples and
ripples up my spine
stimulating
cardiac and mental content
to the heartbeat
and dance   I restrained,
yet survives,
when you cast
me aside   like
I was token,
or teasing.
That which has the strength
to endure
flooding   this shell
in burning torrent,
ripping protection
to shreds of humility.
begging pity

in   uncontrollable
urge   to find
relief from passion
in the folds
of your extremities.
Driving beats
from the left chamber
from   my chest
up my throat
making it impossible
to swallow
past the obstacle
you say doesn't exist—
yet   pounds
moving the
blue   green
Pendleton shirt,
swaddling the
tornado
you overlooked,
in your quest
for someone   to
care for only you
and hold you
above   reason.
Just now   you
appeared   at my
door,   head down,
those incredible
brown eyes raised,
you uttered
"hou."

Wokiksuye

in borrowed language in honor and memory of Bill Ice

Like a horse's tail
so thick, black
down past his waist
beautiful.   Wanyaka.
Chemotherapy—
white man's
man-made cancer . . .
doesn't distinguish
between good or bad
cells . . . just kills.
The spirit is connected
to the hair at the
crown—pahin hocoka.
The hair falls
the spirit goes,
the will is
connected no more.
Leukemia—
cancer of the
White
Blood Cell.
Lakota wicasa
Oglala wica
Ha Luta Oyate   wicozani sni
Kuja, unsika
Canku Wakan o mani
ma wanagi o mani
wasigla
ceya
wokiksuye
wokiksuye
wopilamaye

miksuya
Canku Luta o mani
Canku Waste o mani
wohitika
iyomakpi, iyomakpi
ake—anpetu
anpetu waste
I knew him well.

II

State Of Invisibility

for Janelle and Derya

yellow leaping arrows
expanses
ribs brushing space
emptiness
filling draped skeletal
fashion
herein, the quickened
body sheltering
atom sparks
coffee hour
closer to rise
morning star reach
rattling on deep in
to the night
awaiting dawn
that break of day
forming a line,
blue-white light
on the very border
horizon   to the sun
to the east
to the world
we occur in
and I disappear
forever into crowds
by turning
intentionally to
remain anonymous
save splash colors and
inked pages   torn
to   spread like a fan
to all directions

rippling back the stream
restlessness
meandering minds
holding   then tossing
candlelight   back to
kerosene glass   with
wicks   left   while
surfacing

Darkening Light

for Stephanie

screaming in a voice   not her own
shrills   echo   the parking   lot
as if it were   enclosed   like those downtown underground as if
    it were hollow
as if it held the hollowness she feels this very moment
that great emptiness occurring somewhere deep within   her small
    frame   delicate
features twisted   mouth   eyes   closing blinking bellowing
    as one blows   on a fire
with an instrument resembling the shape of a grand piano but with
    accordion action
that voice it carries the devastation
at least seven lifetimes   maybe eight she is probably very   close to
    nine now
the depth's destruction   blows to souls
within   the slight body   she maneuvers this world in   wavers the mind
    the hollow
life shell vibrates the   meaning   the difficulties
lying underneath the sweetness   it waits   lies   in terror snapping like
    a twig in the palm
a bone in canine jaw   sound waves reverb elongate like the   shutter
    strobes in   old black and white film
HELP   all she ever wanted was to love   to care for   people she was
    closest to and
help   she is flailing fingers   toes   twitch as if it is   a normal reflex
to convulse   spasm   seizure
caesura is all she can hold onto   all the talent she has been credited
    with   that
which could never be stolen   except   by those   she   loved the most
the voice carrying qualities which prick the ear
difficult to discern   to let auditory canal   swallow
she hurls herself toward the other   the passion   the fire itself

that spark   which began   the swing   she just wants to swing so
    high like a child
he grabs her leg   before flight   wings clipped backbone bent
    backward   tears
shoot out from the eye sockets   they spray   rather than slide
    down   out
she   needs out   this world this situation this   life
too many   there can't be a dozen
the cats they   have nine lives   this is what they told her   her
    long hair   swings out
and back in the norther
it gasps   mimicking her own suffering slugs   lung pulls groans
the voice   it shifts   into raspy   throaty   sarcastic pleas   threats
    and repertoire
replay continuing episode series   take   spin-off
look at her separate   dividing
thin line acrobat tightrope display   mental warping
not as bad   is it   as the man with the blue evening gown   reading
    poetry at CCA off sheets as big as posters
not like those   she frequently met who left   the easy way   the way
    that hangs you between worlds
not like the passion on that last voyage   the one where she never
    quite made it back from yet
the one he swiftly carried her into then tossed her out of again
not like them
no   it's not real   stop   it help me stop it she cries
her shoulders hunched and shimmying   shattered distant from
    frontal lobe
the passion claims complete normalcy and says that it was always her
    and never him
she wails   weeping wildly
the parking lot   spins faster than the wheels on the moving vehicles
WHY WHY WHY WHY I never did anything to you she screams
no one touches her no one gives her reason to   breathe
there are no rewards for bad girls
she hears her mother's voice over and over

24

the passion ridicules her pain

he hurries her to his appointment   mustn't be late

she waits   she has nowhere to turn

she spies his legs through the bush   adjusting to please him   the
      legs vanish

she knows he is there   somewhere   avoiding her eyes and her voice
      and the

pulsing drive encaged in rib   it won't stop pounding

she plans in great detail   her   suicide

the ticket purchased when she turned nine   nine lives ago no one
      comes near   no one   checks

on her stability   no one really gives a damn after all   do they

the seekers sought out all they could muster

to list the "incidents" preceding this event this grand finale

nothing was ever   right   never good enough for anything or anyone

especially not the one she devoted herself to

the one that spins castings of flame throwers   circus her mind

the body eating itself in response to the journey   invading cells trigger
      replay relapse

while   he parties with friends and relatives

lodging complaints as to how horrible it really is to be loved by her

dodging insults she lost her balance and lies in a big field of tall
      green grass

The Year of the Rat

for Vaughan and Travis

bu-bon⁻ic plague: a contagious disease characterized
by buboes, fever, and delirium

for days sirens hurl winding shrieks
bubble lights flashing   red   yellow   red
yellow   white   linen
sheets   no,   drapery
rises and settles on
the feet   no, the
hands are pulling it
back again   "can you
hear   us"   they say and
scurry on down the shaolin passageways
the tunnels, or catacombs she lies in
stretch 105 mercury degree rising measure
quicksilver following break
cascading and soaring
could have reached 108
no one knows
faces,   fingers, reappear
pumping machinery
struggling writhing throughout stomach, throat,
eyebrows knitted, pursing lips
blood-drained pallor cheeks they
push and force
tug and pull away plastics
snapping eyes, heels part
fading far farther
white   the tunnels open wide
haunting dark red caverns tiny
obsidian chip eyes peeking through

the watchers   those without fear of man
I can only spectate as
she slips into   recall

dancers   on toe chaotic climax
extremities held in tight circles
bent elbow, dainty toes, black-gray claws
ears slicked back like
a scorned, angered mare
whiskers gleam, tails streaming along to
the dance   the dance
the Mardi Gras
the Coup d'état
the Marathon
They Shoot Horses Don't They?
their bodies wrapped in fur as if they
should be dressed, primped, combed
frenzy filled they   touch lightly   almost
a ballet, or tap, no, free
dance   they are free
from restraints
from being minor mammal
suddenly they huddle
gangly approach to center
like a sneak-up dance
exchanging excitement
they plan,   this is no instinct,
they prepare, premeditate
mutinous recapture of the den
those tunnels outside,   they
were not built by   hares   the
urine odor was not left by infants
dancers left this trace
to forewarn intruders

a single mother, newborn, and infant,
move in escaping her pistol-wielding spouse
lucky to be alive   she tells herself
paying the burly biker landlord
every   dollar she saved
for their escape,   battered, bruised,
splintered dreams,   she cradles both
babies climbing into the green
hand-painted slat board crib
nurses one gives a cracker
to the other

marching onto the so-called shelter
they appear through every
hole in ceiling, wall, and floor
a double dozen, or more,
they make their way into
the rooms   leaping with ease
their foot and foot and a half
from nose to tip of tail   lengths
lumbering onto shelves,
formica counters,   the one antique
dresser riddled with wormholes,
teeth gnaw continuously   turning
solid matter to Swiss cheese in the
den, the sheetmetal mobile home

the mother covers the sleeping
innocents   she clutches an empty   2-liter glass
Coke bottle in the right hand
and iron claw hammer with rough, splintered
wooden handle   in the left   she
tells the pack, the herd, the congregation
these are her children
she says this with her eyes
she wedges herself into the corner of the crib

staying guard through
weary length of night, she
swings on occasion when
one ventures close—range
hoping to take a finger as
the lost child from Birdtown lost toes
to these   years ago   gnawing, growing
teeth   in hopes of taking
the taste of milk
from sleeping baby lips
she connects at least twice each night
she never sleeps
the nightmares allow the rulers victory
dragging bones, her children's, from their teeth
like game trophies to be hung below floors
she dozes midday   in the
car with no gas and no floorboard
her babies tied to her
she never sets them down

"They are like tigers" her
dad told her "never corner them,
they become as panthers,
as Bengals" he told her long   ago
she wishes he had a
phone   or that she had one
to get a message to him
that he was right   that they
are here to prey on the
living, larger mammals   man
she remembers her mother's screams
at walls and stove ventilation
raving conversation with tormentors
no one else could see
and leaving at thirteen
her brother pounding her face

with fists and pool balls
his favorite hobby
her father hard at work every day
as if he could work away the madness
her sister fleeing six weeks before
packing one suitcase as if it were an overnight
remembering the way she said
"when they dance, they have it"
she knows this true   firsthand,
she observes performance
the ritual
it terrifies her
the dance, the dance, bounding, leaping closer
here, she defends the trench of trailer,
the foxhole crib they lie in
while the rulers plan strategies
and taunt her

amazed at their aggressiveness
she wishes for a gun,
or knife,   a better implement
to fight with during this
night they are especially
close   the light,   that one
single line,   precise between earth
and sky   both pitch
that clear blue white line appears
to break day,   crows caw
outside   the owls   make roosting sounds
the watchers chew and twitch before
jumping to floor, scattering
to holes and scampering out of light
into the ground   tunnels
into the underground
the den beneath this floor
like vampires retiring to mausoleums

to choreograph the "ring around the rosy"
for the new dusk to come
den of daytime
they sink into tunnels
like bats   in daylight
with the same ammonia-filled stench

the young mother
closes her eyelids momentarily
only to seal them slightly
the pull so taut
black rings below   she
slides over the crib railing
releasing bottle and club   no,
hammer   she thought it
a club   wish splitting manifestation
she changes babies and feeds
them   all she can
then bundles them
and ties them to herself
her sister once called her a pack-mule
babies cling like koala bear clip-ons
they know nothing of the danger
she raises them from
she wraps a big
towel around the three of them
covering her shoulders
with a faded car coat
they leave the
den   leave the lights on
repelling rodents
in their absence
they walk
the small mother
carrying the full
load of three

kicking stones
along the way
remembering days before
days of war on homefronts
racing from attacks
knowing that for her
there is nowhere safe to run
a single brown sedan
flies by them   on the long
stretch of highway
they amble alongside of
between steps they sigh
the gravel thickens
as they reach the country store
the wooden ramp under her feet
they enter

making way to shelving, hunting
hardware,   holding   careful watch
they locate traps
twelve inches long
she lifts four and then
four again,
lays eight on counter
she pleads for credit writing
promise on colored paper
the owner looks at her
at the traps
looks at her again
double-take
spine erect
she loads courage
in her eyes   agreement
reached, she raises the bag
he dropped them into
retrieving the items to count

eight   she works up a pressed
curve of lip into slight smile
they

return, armed
the babies know nothing   she thinks
and tells herself
she's doing all she
can to take care of them and at
least their father can't kill her   now
she is bigger than these dancers
these new adversaries   these
barons of the earth almost
as ancient as the roach   though
twice as evil
she imagines them
tremendous dragons
and plans masquerading carnival
invitational trap   once
again   inside the den
mobile home

the trailer is decorated in Early American cardboard
she never unpacked on seeing the rats
the tiny woman gathers boxes,   these boxes
she sets in appropriate positions,
vantage points, they secure
at night she places scoops
of commod peanut butter and oil
on the traps' triggers and pulls
back the springs   tucking in
tongue catch,   setting force,   she lays
them ever so gently   deep inside
corrugated cubes
ripping newspaper
hoarded in her car trunk

to shreds
she gently, ever so
gently   lets the shreds and strips
fall   like crumbs of snow from her fingers
filling entirely the space above
the bottom, center-squared   sharply pulling
back her hands to let them
"lie in peace"
masquerading as nesting
materials   for those who come
at night   for their underworld
home   below her feet
and the crib's
legs

the sky outside casts
over   deepest gray, telltale coal
clouds surround the meadows   out
in the open
lightning time
begins
the strikes stab sky
bolting toward the metal walls
and roof   she quickly places the
babies into high chairs   the chairs' legs
safely set into eight decaying
sneakers   four under each chair
the pots and pans
on the steel stove top
dance   from surges
untamed electricity
lights the burners
all four knobs read OFF
over orange-red coils bouncing cookware
the dead motor
in the air conditioner

buzzes, jars, and tries to turn over
though when she turned it ON
herself this strain never occurred
light bulbs   hanging exposed from the ceiling
glow brighter with each lightning stroke
charges ignite and leap at times from sockets
the rubber soles of old
shoes   protecting babies   barely
she has done this before
stranded during storms in previous escapes
her husband always found her
as if his sonar hits
were more direct than lightning
the baby caught in everything
then there was one, now there are two
the three a family
by blood and flesh
clap and crash   thunder pounds
sheet walls shimmy
vibrating from pressure and forces living, ruling
eventually the rains join the streaks
and dance in electrical fallout
the drops and sparks   fire and
water

she sweeps the floor
watching the window   the black dung
pellets left overnight flying out the
doorway   day passes like all the
rest   this year   the dancers will
spin years of dreams   night terrors
dark cyclones filled with black eyes
scraping, gnawing, teeth   but
that is far into the future
she is here in the now
shadows skip sundial   night

falls as a shade
night shade
night watch
the dancers clamber
out of chambers onto the
porch   out of the sliding glass
doors   she carries the babies
to the bright green crib   and
lulls them to sleep
Indian songs she sings
she cradles them
in her arms until the slumber
is sufficient to last the night
time   she takes the bottle that
glass 2-liter   in her right
and the iron claw hammer
in her left and makes   ready
she catches the dancers bounding
so elegantly, so gracefully
she catches sight
and smell of the
dancers

they   watch her as
well   creeping closer together
they huddle tails entwined
they scheme, slink away,
file into formations
taking the walls,
floors and ceiling   by storm
combative stances
they laugh her off
through the night she connects
a few again   though they relish
their glory   as kings   she
nothing but a damsel

the largest dancer
a gift from Europeans
giant from Norway—the
King   he is a tyrant and always
taunting her   this time they
get bored   in this game and leap
showing off their egos inflated
they bound into boxes to
play with shredded stuffing and
quench the desire for
government-issue
peanut butter
        trigger snaps
tongue catch   and springs   f l y
sending steel   over
backs and   bones   and
fur   four times   then
rear lines   follow   four
more snaps   the others
have no heart for fallen fellows
and continue the taunting closeness
edging   toward   her babies
dodging glass and hammer   claw
the game so merrily played
throughout the hours in this
night   in the long
month of September   this
time she feels some sort of
security

when crack-light
dawn breaks the still sky
the survivors retreat   she
lifts the first box   the
rodent's dead weight
makes her sick

even though she
cannot see it through the
shredded papers   still filling
space   covering the body
weight and smell fill her
with fear that it will jump
toward her sight unseen
and lay its fangs into her
skin   she casts the box
at least twenty feet out
the door

she slowly walks
over to inspect its contents
the cadaver lies   back broken
twelve or more inches long
she wants to throw up but
has no time   all the others
sail out into the meadow
because each time she feels
their dead weight her arms
uncontrollably fling boxes
one by one until
eight are spread

hours later she recovers
the shock initial
and begins releasing traps to reset
peanut butter surprise
she washes her hands and
arms   for forty minutes
straight   before caring for
the children, for the day
the children know nothing, they're so
innocent, they don't know anything
it is so still, the wind drifting stench

is the only movement   the sky
remains dark, blackest black
gray-tipped lining cloud
boxes, traps, shreds,
boxes, traps, shreds
she commits to the order
front line in corrugated mine field
snap, spring, dancers fall
the flank moves forward

the landlord comes one day
when he arrives she cries   to
him begging for abatement
rent   on the den   he laughs
her off   his ears look like
the king's—pointed   she steals
serial number from his
work truck to garnish his
wages in court   she will sue
she says   he backhands
her   just as her husband did
so many times before   she
left him in June   paid the
rent three months' advance
to this wannabee slumlord
single dwelling dictator
this leech of land-
lord-ing   now the winter is
approaching fast   the babies notice
and cry they notice
they are aware
time is running   out

the owner of the store
is surprised to see her
he agrees to take her to town to file

small claims court   in a few weeks
the landlord tells the judge
that the reason the rats came
was because of her housekeeping

"No.   They were already here."
she says showing pictures of rats in
traps   she drew to scale
the babies crawl around the
courtroom   the people stare
and shake their heads   they judge,
they convict,   they send her to
jail   in their minds   "Your Honor,
it's the truth"   she says and he
allows her to reclaim one hundred dollars
suggesting she "look better
next time you rent" her shoulders
rise and tighten, lips part
salted words dissolve on her tongue
the babies scamper around
till they locate her legs
and climb
up to be held tight

a singer she knows tells her about
a basement apartment,
fixer-up rental they collapse
into   it smells sweet   they eat and
sleep   night passing   something
scratches and runs   in the
false ceiling   she sees black
eyes   in her mind   she hits
the white, dusty panels
and a possum falls
almost into her arms
she screams, then laughs hysterically

they get a cat, a real mouser
the feline patrols every night
protecting the babies
they sleep on a mattress
no longer in a crib
there are no shadows
from slats on their faces   babies
turn into tots and play
she writes songs
gathering random chords
prays to be left alone
and prays not to be lonesome
she falls to sleep writing and smiling
at her children

she dreams
she is in the tunnels of the
rulers   former terrorists   *who
was the tenant?*   this question
in dreamscape

her body becomes ridden with pain
sickness so strong
fever shoots so high
nothing can bring it down

five days have passed
amnesia, the sickness reels, she tries to cry
but her lips won't work
she lies in her own vomit
her hand reaches out with effort
to the silhouette of the younger child
she contacts dry parched skin like old
paper   paper-thin leather, fragile gray
her skin is also gray   she
can see it   the older child

across her feet both children out
cold   dying   or already gone
she cannot move
darkness, quiet silence, death is coming
she smells it and turns away
to turn,   to f a l l
to fall to the floor   she crawls
like the babies to the wall   she
cannot reach   the phone
she pushes open the door and falls

out into the cold
the fierce cold of this winter
her fever melts the snow next to
her gray, gray skin   schoolchildren
stumble across her body   and run
for help down the dirt road
they scurry
their mother lifts her into their
wagon   station wagon   they lay
her babies beside her in the back
Is this a hearse?
the clinic doctor will not
allow them within doors   "No way,
they are gray, look at them."
He covers his mouth and face with enormous hands
the strangers drive an hour to a
Public Health Service Hospital
and leave the three behind as they
hurry home for supper

the tiniest on saline intravenous
once he can speak
the biggest child tells the story
of the last five days

he fed the baby   while his mother
lay dying   "I thought she would
died" he says   explaining that after the third day
he couldn't feed the baby and crawled in with
her   he saw the baby crawl in the fourth day
"I think it was yesterday, dunno"
in another room she is told "They will make it,
you didn't lose your children."
"Can you hear us?"

the tunnels close
in around her the glass beads
black,   those eyes   like size
ten seed beads   glassy, shiny
they watch her, they rule

      I

have witnessed all of this from
far   above   this
plague-ridden   room   floating
around   I feel free   enough to

dance

      I

look back at she

once   I suppose   was me
too difficult   I decide
and watch a little longer   I slip in above
the babies
I know they need her to come back
delirious she yells "What's the cover routine?"
those hands slip a needle
to vein   she jerks   I jerk
with   her   and reclaim   the body

while the mind encounters steely eyes

dancers

plague dreams,   reality
leaping,   flying,   scampering
gnawing innocents
good healthy bodies
tearing away the escape of a lifetime
those tunnels   full to brim
rodents racing   through time
through this year   the fever

falls

chills rise my skin
bead goose bumps, my mind
is clearing   "Are the dancers gone?
Are the babies okeh?"   Hands and
faces embody nurses, doctors

"Have you had any recent contact
with any small animals?" they ask

recall dancers on toe   chaotic climax frenzy
they   dance   the dance   they dance

III

Shoe Gestapo at the Blue Light Special Place

for Ruth Mustus and Garth Lahren

Blue Light Special Place
Indian Heaven
innocently Stoney Woman picks up
a pair of shoes for her niece
checks in to check-out counter
scanners beep and register difference in price
accusatory insults flash in clerk's light eyes
shoe gestapo summoned and arrives in authoritative walk
customer's growing concern, impatience, and popping sweat
gestapo checks down pricing charts
friend to Stoney Woman demands explanation
Shoe Gestapo Man of the Blue Light Special Place
whispers, "How are You?"
"All right! Mr. Authority's a Skin, too!"
checking chart with concealed smile
she's cleared
she's relieved
check-out girl sneers anyway

Night In Chaos

for Sandy Hinkle and Clay Woody

Tires squealing
like rubber screams
fire flashing
from the barrel
A few choice words of English
in a barrage of Spanish
Blinds rise and slide open
faces peer into the night
Babies cry from jolted sleep
and boys run across the streets
looking at broken glass and metal
Where ARE the mothers?
I hate you! I'm going to kill you!
No, I'm going to kill you!
Puta, BITCH, STUPID MOTHERFUCKING BITCH!
No, Don't . . . DON'T, please, ple—
Screaming of a different kind
Stucco and window shatter interrupting
private affair with gang warfare
flashing from low-rider's cherry ride
escalating terror
she looks for her make-up

Responses

for Betty Holyan and Susan Power, ACA suvivors

skin light, tinged yellow-olive
sharp ridge bone top cheeks
tassel strands spinning gold, gold,
scalloped backs of frontal teeth
laced tennis shoes outside
wrapped feet turned forever in
integrated world
sovereign traditional culture
dominant language
indigenous language
forget the past
you are the past
one and the same
specific result
of   interracial marriage
product parcel
of   modern man
one strangles
one survives
I am a survivor
I know who I am
myself, I know
you ask outright
"Were you raised by Indians?"
"How do you know those songs?"
"How can this be?"
I confuse you   and
in your confusion
you demand
far past my visual perceptions
through me   not   at me
past me   not   here

where I am
"There must be   some
mistake."   you say
I politely   and   not so politely
inform you
that this is what happens
when you snag a skin
for experimental purposes
for the "Native American Experience"
and your own flesh and blood offspring
cannot survive in your world
the world you manifested for yourself
your own child   belongs
to another world,   another way,
and you may never come into
that world   no matter how
hard you coerce
it is a simple matter of blood
and culture   conveniently deny
you have your own
you must be ashamed, I guess, by now
but you cannot fix it
by stealing more of mine
it's just not for sale
it never really was
nor will it ever be
you marvel at my poetry techniques
and how on earth this
breed woman-child
can take a simple menu
and read:

Famous Burger
Greek Salad
French Fries

Toasted American Cheese Sandwich
Fish on a Bun
Top Sirloin Butt Steak
Chicken Parmesan
Breaded Veal Dinner
Chop Sirloin
Flounder Dinner
Shakes

can take your trash
and furnish a life
can take so much   and
dare explode on select occasion
and yet   you   take and take and take
and want more
you   who created
my   people's struggle
and my own personal interracial existence
some of your very own people   sometimes
treat me as a human being
not as an oddity, a curio,
not expecting me to pass
—as if I would ever even want to be you—
but   to accept that I am   different
and they are few
and I am many
we are the mixed-bloods
the war babies
and conceptions of more humanistic humans
or so we would like   to believe
and intend to
the breeds   and even those
far removed métis and mestizos
who would like to forget both
sides of themselves

and create a new "modern" version of culture
but I myself, I refuse to accept
less than the utmost
satisfaction in surviving
in your wannabee world
no matter what the cost
rather than sell out
exploit, forget, pass off . . .
if you miss me
you missed the boat
maybe on the way to America
land of the free
for some
for your great white hope
not for me
or maybe on your way to
Indian Country
to snag your own personal skin
I know for you it's all smoke
in your blindness   don't ever
confuse white with red
you might miss the boat

Sidelays Gwance

for Sandy

Noose slips
swings loosely
preceding
White Man's lodge
Again   the
megalomania
mediacentric
flash   snap and tape
documenting
documented peoples
those peoples   registered
to the Department of Interior
along   side
wild   life,   wild-er-ness
those wild   people
refusing to remain
under pacification
undermining dominant
society's dogma
mining,   always mining,
Again reversing   throw
bark to blade
relocating,   reallocating lives
attempting snare
spirituality snare
their game denied
she dangles by
jawline   strangle vine
accepting new road death
rather than selling
ghosts to hosts
claiming new age obligations

Pleas

for Charmaine and all the res children

Guided by
learned behavior.
rung on ladder,
score on page,
chapter in book.
Destined   children,
future generations,
the lucky ones,
unaffected by
FAS .... FAE
search as their
parents   once searched
for the warriors
for the strong women
accomplished and respected
to mother and father them.
THE ORPHANS
of assimilation   and
of the drink of
dissension, weakness,
and misery.
If strength and wisdom
are to be reclaimed
and justice committed,
who among us stands
to fill   the   empty   role?

Compartmentalizing

for Molly Bigknife Shackleford &
Gino Antonio, J. Crews, E. Fragua, & E. Morrison

Compartmentalizing   acknowledged correlations.
Linkage of fibers   weaving mainstream   tapestry,
containing proud   Americans'   historical
    accomplishments,
   . . . .
1890 . . . leading national heroes
organize   apple pie, hot dogs,   and the Brooklyn
    Dodgers.
Compartmentalizing   unacknowledged correlations.
Trail of   frayed promises   tearing apart survival,
way of life,   devastating proud   Native Peoples'
respectful accomplishments

   . . . .
1890 . . . leading national heroes
organize   theft,   genocide,   and such massacres as
    Wounded Knee.
Compartmentalizing   mainstream Americans,
continue to claim . . .   in complete undying faith . . .
no current correlation to   crimes committed
by the   perpetrators   of   Manifest Destiny
guaranteed by the biblical prophets' historical page
in belief that these Americans were   a different people
The United States of America, based on religious freedom
and shopping malls

   . . . .
1776 . . . Native Freedom of Religion Act delayed until
    1978 . . . Medals and honors bestowed upon the 7th
    Calvary match in
correlation to those bestowed upon the Brooklyn Dodgers.
Apple pie,   hot dogs,   baseball,   heroes,   and genocide.
Product and part   of the   assembly line accomplishments of

historical value in Mainstream American pride.
. . . .
1990 . . . leading national heroes
take Indian names, claim reincarnation from Native spiritual
    leaders,
mimic war cries during ball games . . .
Redskins, Braves, Warriors, Chiefs . . .
parody sacred ceremony in automotive industry
Sundance, Thunderbird, Cherokee Chief, Dakota, Cheyenne . . .
Is compartmentalization   technique   in assimilation,
in destruction,   in persecution?

We the People, united we stand . . . words taken directly from
    Native constitution
    from sea to polluted sea.
. . . .

Legacy

(dual-voice performance piece)
for Chris Apache & Chris, Michael, & Lisa Brooks

in 1992

> Surviving in the post-
> traumatic era in
> the dark ages following
> the systematic genocidal
> encroachment of the
> displaced invaders,
> intruders, currently
> occupying and implementing
> martial   law throughout
> the western hemisphere

Bob HedgeCoke
All you eastern hemisphere
people   are   just alike

They expect us   to believe
Europe and Asia   are   N O   A D C
separate continents
and that we walked across   N O   B I A
from over there
or   that space   N O   C I B
invaders built   our
pyramids and
medicine wheels   N O   S E R V I C E
for us

Bob HedgeCoke
Good thing we had

fish on hand
you might have
starved

So, your ancestors
were fresh off the
boat, huhn,   the
Mayflower, huhn,
mine were here to meet them

    Dehl Berti
Smallpox, measles, typhoid,
TB, syphilis—all of
these   we acquired
in exchange for
a pair of glasses

Booze, alcohol   the
s l o w   smallpox blanket
we are still trying
to uncover its
disastrous effects

Hudson Bay Blankets
    &
Hudson   Bay Rum

    Ban the Booze   in
Indian Country
Abolish the s l o w   trade
    blanket

That old man   you called a
    drunk,
      dirty   Indian
is my father.   He never did take
the drink you poured down my
throat.   Your manager said he
could get these boxes in the

alley   to pack some   things in
            that
we are moving. That man has a
        college education.
He grew up in a dugout,
        in the 1920s.
He fought with honors in your
        World War II.
He went to medical school
riding fence to   pay   in Grand
        Forks
before there was an INMED.
        He
worked for your Agriculture
Department, for your
Helium Research,   for your NASA,
        for the
EPA   until you gave him
bronze medals and claimed we
no longer needed environmental
protection.   That man knows
our old ways   and your new way
that you   yourself
are too slow and stupid to
grasp.   You'd better watch who
you call   dirty and drunk that's
my father.   He bathed in rivers
        while
you powdered yourself to hide
        your smell.

It's a computer pow wow
Japanese Apple Macintosh
Hey,   what's that?
Hey, come check this out.
What is that?
Hey, this pow wow's
points   are added up
on a laptop computer.
Looks like a toy.
Hey, get over here.
Dancers be on the floor
at 1:30 Macintosh
Time.   No, not Indian Time.
Japanese computer time.
Grand Entry at 1:30
Macintosh Pow Wow Time.
Institute of American Indian
        Arts
Thirtieth Anniversary   1962-1992
Spring Celebration Pow Wow
I hear that the Writing Majors
protested for these computers
It's about time   we got hold of
some choice equipment.

we used to say   every ridge
don't spin webs   a bone
the white man says   every peak
don't spin wheels   a vertebra
we turn that around   rising,   forming
and say   to our   your skeleton
young   following every
spin creations   mound and crevasse

I see
your spirit
living

standing   upon
your skin
I feel
my spirit
living, too

That Diné
man
he   stumbled blinded
right across   the
Santa Fe Rail
looking   for the
curb   shop
in Gallup.
That white man shot him
said he thought   he
was   a   deer.

I am a young woman
I respect my elders
I follow my heart
and   use my mind   to
benefit my community.
I am a single mother.
I respect my children.
I nurture their talents
and encourage them to
use their minds
to benefit their community

Our mother is crying
Our grandfather
he looks at us
and he cries, too

The principles we were raised
        with
in a good way,   as females,   as
        Indians:
generosity, empathy,
        compassion, loyalty.

Today due to
the monumental
change inflicted upon us
by the European transplant society
mark us   like   targets
to be used, cruised, abused,
conned, and taken advantage of
even by   some of our
own   people

Continue on
on the other side
your walk
will be remembered
honored, respected.
Even   when   the endurance
is all winter after   winter
all that really matters
is that you help
someone   somewhere
along   your   path
grow
Physically, mentally,
emotionally, or spiritually,
even by laying
           a hand on the shoulder
of a crying   stranger
and praying in   your
mind
You can help by
turning   tears
to   smiles   and
laughter

M. Bull Bear
A warrior helps an old person,
a child, a single woman.
A warrior is not someone
with braids, sunglasses,
and a cool statement

64

Bob HedgeCoke
Phil Sheridan   was
the hard enemy
he put the bounty
on the buffalo
Custer was nothing
but a rapist and baby killer

You better be careful
if you say the truth
the Feds will have
to kill you

I wish I never told you
as much as I did
now you're a threat
you know too much

Defend your people
Defend our way of life
Be willing to give your life
to do these things

if   the time
        is right
grow
        and help others
grow
        and your tears
can also
turn to smiles
and laughter
rather than

falling rain
from the old
ones   crying
above
continue on
They told us that
this generation would
eat our children
What they meant
was that our men
would take our ADC
and drink it up and use it
for gas and leave
        us and our kids
hungry and without.

One hundred thousand American
        Indians
reside in Los Angeles and
greate   L.A.   No greater concentration

65

in an urban community   may be
found in the United States, even
        almost
as large as the population
on the Diné reservation, Navajos
I went into the PHS   in
Ventura County   just next
door to L.A.   and   there was
no box that said   American Indian
or Native American   on the form.
        Once
again I checked off OTHER,
once again   I got angry,
once again   I understood,
this is our land,   our health care
We are   yet   OTHER
        only to you   and
        your voice of   justice

F. Thunder Hawk
For them only
They say it means
justice   just-us

The only forms I found
with a box   that identified
Native peoples   were
in Indian organization
offices,   where there were
no   other   choices
other than to modify
        descriptives.
When   there is no alternative,
no choice,
modification   only   is

offered, only modification
No solution No resolution
        Breaking waves
Thundering brain waves
pound in cranial capacities
and migraine me   back home.

If   they truly respected
Crazy Horse   they would
simply name a mountain
for him and leave the
physical form   pure
rather than blasting
it into a replica
supposedly of him,
he who had no picture ever
        taken.

in 1492

IV

When I Was a Girl Woman

for Marguerite and Betty

When I was a girl woman, early on, late in my teens.
When I had already been married three years, two years
    longer than any other my same age,
I felt as free, flowing, and proud as the waving purple flags, irises,
growing deep beside concrete block steps splashed well over with
    white latex paint.
        Back when I planted gardens and crops to live by,
          rather than just to survive
and I recognized the deep purple blooms of my teens as
    the offspring of an iris I had planted
  in a red Folger's can,
    second grade sometime.
Remembering how it was my first bulb, a purple iris I
    carried like a newborn infant home from grade school.
Proud, when from the wet earth, spooned in with
    sterling silver serving spoons,
spoons I'd pried from the same ground I dug dirt from
    to fill the class-assigned container, coffee tin.
When from dampened dirt there erupted stiff green shoots,
    proper positioning, buried bulb.
Proud, as if somehow, somewhere inside me shoots were
    stabbing through soil, fanning out, standing straight.
One center shoot a rounder stem which would bud and
    flower deep grape purple.
Pollen-tasseled-lined petals captivating orange
    spider-webbed wings fluttering by,
proud monarch butterfly enticed by waxy soft petals
    which made my own mouth water though I chose
    wild rose petals to swallow, their taste perfuming
    my tongue and texture deep satisfaction for girl
    woman curiosity.

When I was a girl woman,
I moved as gracefully as gladiolus sway in slight breeze.
Gladiolus like those I grew gently near flagstone
    walkway, surrounded by big, black tractor tires,
    and around a pale   cornerstone.
Blooms stacked upon stem, layers overlapping, as if they
    were drapery curls or
ruffles on chiffon bed skirts or short, sassy skirts
    decorating young girls from the whiter section of growers.
Those growers down the road, farther down from my small
    yellow house,
down the path I stepped lightly upon, dressed in straight
    cotton shifts or Levi's, on the way to pick blackberries,
    or scuppernongs,
those wild grapes with outer skins, skins so thick you had to
    peel them off to enjoy the sweet, wet fruit inside.
        Skins that seemed to forbid discovery.
On the road where I placed toe-heel precision in canter walk
    much like the
simple filly dance on that chestnut I found at fifteen,
    dangling broken hemp and halter,
the one nobody claimed.   I staked her near garden beds,
away from fields, sweet potatoes and tobacco, nearer
    winter rye grass planted closer for cattle graze.
I touched earth with precision and respect the way little
    girls jingle dress dance   dainty, bubbly.
But, sometimes the way the ruffled edge of river water
    rolls foam   turning childlike to full grown   character
as complicated as the filly's own conditional personality,

"Yes, you may catch me   if your hands are full of
    licorice root, anise leaf, and you approach me
    walking backward singing 'Grandchild, come with
    me' in Indian."
"No, you cannot catch me   I am like the cloud horse
    chasing stallions across blue pasture above,"

above those peach gladiolus, multitudes bound by
        singular umbilical stem which together became beautiful bouquet,
my favorite flowers of all.

When I was a girl woman I looked through lace curtains
as if lying in green grass looking up through Queen
        Anne's lace, hovering at the edges of the yard.
Flowers framing boundaries converting ordinary field
        rye to lush rye grass of lawns.
Where black swallowtails' caterpillars crawled every spring
to feed on ivory and green and milkweed in between
        lace-patterned growth.
Like the patterned treetops which bustled through lace
        curtains, lemon gold and lime green, cradling mistletoe
which I shot out with .410 birdshot, trying my best to
        shoot as sharp as my paternal grandmother
who could shoot so straight and clean she tossed six black walnuts
        in the air
and popped each one with the six-shooter she drew from
        underneath her bright blue shawl.
The same story was talked around about a distant cousin's grandma.
That cousin who was the Indian Secret Service bodyguard to
        Roosevelt
not like those of us in tradition but a Bible thumper,
        yet his grandmother as sharp a shot as my own.
Through lace curtains I witnessed sunlight transform into shadow
        roses and ribbons through delicate weave.
Roses sweeping walls inside   kitchen, bath.
Shadow flowers moving through the day
as light rolls blue pasture seeking horses and girls gone astray.

As tough as dun and paint mustangs I green and gentle broke
and as steel plows I broke earth with, its brown waves
        cresting like the ocean, plowed into furls by a ship,
throwing the old ones' arrowheads and spear points, from long ago,

onto the topsoil from three feet below.
As tough as the jays stealing nuthatch eggs,
so swollen with mischief they cry out in laughter, mocking even me.
I was as aware as the sensitivity plant, low to ground in rye,
green and touchy little leaves cluttered down a single spine.
As aware as the pine needles forgotten on ground wishing they were
    woven baskets.
As aware as the heron piercing ponds across the fields for sunfish
    and bluegills.
As aware even as the fish waiting to throw themselves to the brim
    of water, as prey.

When I was a girl woman I was different.
While most others dreamed in their sleep, I dreamed in
    my wakefulness.

While everyone ran from the "horned demon," the only one I
    ever saw in my life,
that all the other field-workers and barn hands wanted to squash
    the life out of,
grabbing tobacco sticks and axes to club and divide it to death,
    while they ran and armed themselves   I studied
this eight-inch caterpillar and marveled over its face painted brilliant
    in neon by nature
as a great dragon like the Chinese might use overseas
Blue, yellow, crimson dazzled me and I carried the lepidopteran
    far from those, tabooed by memory,
by days of "horned demon" bounty and glory in cotton fields,
    now planted shoulder deep in bright leaf tobacco.

Where other brides spent earnings on Hershey's candy
    bars and store-bought clothes
I cooked caramel candy on the stove and sewed all our clothes
    by hand, except for blue jeans,
and spent the earnings I made to travel to places I'd missed and
    those I'd never seen.

74

I was so different when I was a girl woman that I didn't even know
      any other girl women,
just gray-haired grandmas in printed calico and lively little girls
      in covered rubber band ponytails and braids,
those I could learn from and those I could teach.

There's so much to the girl woman world, those of us who leave it
      far behind forget most of what it holds.

But, when I was a girl woman I was only practicing

and when I get really old, I mean older than the boundaries marked
      on the fields, older
      than the garden's rows,
I'll be so good at it, from choosing to remember all I have learned,
I just might be a woman girl.

Perheron Nambe Morning

for Travis and Vaughan and
all the St. Catherine's Indian School kids

dust, leaves twirling
whirlpool
up off road
under wheels
undercarriage
automotive   winds
turning,   lifting
giving force to such
delicate   particles
ends attached in former
position to branch
soft paper thin petal-
like reds and golds
much as the mane swings
blows back   from higher
plane winds   Percheron   gold
mane   that red Percheron
on the right
the north side
you've seen her
in the early morning
when it's snowing she
raises her dignity
laughing at motorists
distressed by ice
and Pueblo patrol cars
we catch in peripheral
focus   signal   turn the
halogens off and on
on and off   until
they code the signal

distress signal
approaching tribal police
traffic trap
commuting   the
35 mph racket
through Nambe
Pojoaque turn   50
Tesuque Bingo/Pull-Tabs
long before the lodge
turned stone   near Camel Rock
before the Congested Area in
approach to the
"City of the Oldest Catholic Church in North America"
we convey these
danger signs   to
local yokels   perhaps even
tourists   if we're in mood
consideration
strange nation
neither of us belong
though   we do stay
in close   proximity to
these other   Native peoples
very different than where we
come from   still the same
only *sometimes*   though
they know the patrol
man he's their cousin
all of theirs
they know this whirl
these leaves   rising now
before our heated grill
Chevy 4x   '91
they know the Percheron
she steals the scenery easily
with her laughter and turn

pitching hoof and tail
in mockery   indispensable humor
she takes this morning
under gray the shade of nickel
to cloud the stress enabling
me to speak to you of
beauty

Look At This Blue

In my eye
the surging
tides well
beyond
control recoil.
They fill
lapping over,
lashes flicker,
and seal
the angle
of focus,
the flash
of light refraction—
lens mirrored—
structure your face.
I see brilliant
creation
lingering
on   fine thread.
Capacity
to link
passageway
between   us   two.
A shirt quivers,
trembling blades of shoulder
designing   collar
and stretch.
I reach further,
into strands
of honor and respect.
Desire quickens,
you flinch
and chide   my

sincere extreme
intention.
Fingertip   brushing
your skin,
the drop rolls
my cheek.
I close   the
damage
and   dream
you   put   aside
your hesitancy
kissing away
waters
before I slip
and   drown.
The kingfisher
visits your irises.

Sequinned

for S. J. in the city & Marsha Stands

Don't tell me you couldn't reach down pick up
the whole gleaming garment and wear it
to fancy shawl dance back home.   Dancing proud
in a twenty-four-dollar trinket city

all laid out
shimmering and shining on jet black world
traffic lights, street lamps, hot neons, cool fluorescents.

Headlights
    swim freeways electric

    minnows, glittering eyelets on bridges
bridges lacing up New York and Newark, separate
sides of a sequinned vest.   Borough lights trace out
webbed wing

butterfly designs, no wasps—mosquitoes even.
Something ready to fly off the whole metro stretch.
Some cousin calling:

Girl, leave your French braids tight   'cause
    Cut Nose is goin' ta have it out with you
over snagging her sometimes half-side last night.
She wants to take your prize and crown
    from Red Nations Pow Wow—

Her eyes painted sharp red at the corners,
red as the landing light
    on this plane's wing tip.
Her plume high and straight, the Empire State,
while yours falls
    gently over your part.   But that vest—

red, green, gold, silver sparkles,
no one's got more brilliance.
More elegant than bugle beads and embroidery,
more stunning than satin and silk.

Girl, don't you let that city get away.
Lift it up, raise it, slip your arms through
and take it back to dance.

Pine Ridger With a Lamborghini Dream

Ricochet   you   Pine Ridger with a Lamborghini dream
share with me this insight   this exquisite   invisible rainbow
stretched before this South Dakota truck across postcarded southwest
where I develop affection for curvaceous narrow road
almost abandoned to romance by   haunting recollective
     psychotic alcoholic
                  episode
they moved the mare that captured me   between those
     highway maps'
                  insignificant color lines
she's gone   but somehow   you and me   get *somehow* we
     linger on   together
capturing innermost desirous feelings
fleeting   always   fleeting   *in a special kind of way* they endure
look   the single star   to the southwest   lighting the night sky
over the fiery sundown horizon   cedar and juniper blackened by
     loss of reflection
drop night shade to dark   cobalt to midnight blue   unaffected by
emerald go lights   or caution amber   hills darker without tungsten
outshining stars against the pitch of sky   spaced   matched equally
black   black light   blacklight   bugcatching device
black to conceal   to reveal   you   shimmering black sea
     pinpricked holes spark   shimmer
cottonwood creating lace patterning webbing alcoves space
     in between more
                  branched lace
across yellow orange moon   ridge across this path pathways
     to parts of me
I honestly forgot existed   the most secluded and denied
     essential components   depth   me
willingly drawn   shades open   by chord   your mood evokes
to dwindle only you   I spin the hydraulic tool   the jack
     you drug out   changing

                    blown-out Firestone
        alongside woven wood   branches   wire warp pueblo fencing
            we swerved toward
        while my pen covered contemplation   one boy's braid flowing past
            his narrow hips
        kicking gravel   the other attempting performance
            macho masquerading
                            mechanical knowledge
        both cold, tired   jet black   surrounding over, above, and
            across sparkle and
                        surrender lighting
        automotive lamps passing   offering solution to dilemma
            somewhere near Cundiyo
                        and so on
        the nearly 4'4" mechanic younger boy   who originated
            the Lamborghini dream
                        stooping low
        beside you   "Watch the traffic"   I beg and return to   pen on the
            blue seat of the
                        white and black truck
        much better than the older Datsun with formica and
            plywood floorboards that
                        flooded out over rain-filled potholes

        currently without the familiar fear of frostbite in the colder months
            approaching
                        fast
        already the brilliant casts of snow-dusted lower slopes remind us
            mountains
                        without fear   further   without the
        fear of exposure caused alcoholic frozen death grips
            unless, of course, we
                        surrender to fixate certain   relapse
        tendencies attributed to atrocities   freely now made into

        84

a give-away

        we no longer hold dear

nor cling to   shimmer slow into   this night falling   into this
clearing cross section

        in our individual paths

in night without fear   without solitude   yet comfortable
belonging   glimmering   sparkle shining by   breathe

Radio Wave Mama

for my mother Hazel who lost remembering,
and for those close who can't forget

transistor radios
planted firmly
against ears
the children
smothered under
pillows over
their   heads   and
shoulders
escaping the sounds of "ssssss"
and vulgarities screamed
they didn't know the
true meaning of
and invented   replacement
definitions   from
expansive imaginations
when the vocal tensions   invaded
the safer   place
of refuge
under covers
over lumps   in
shared bed they composed
songs to   avoid
rhythms of madness
and poems to
describe hysteria   or
to rearrange
perspectives   of   life
their life
their metaphoric
existence
cropped by

delusions
when the wrath
dispensed   overflow
they crawled on
the floor
before school and
scrubbed the baseboards
with toothbrushes
and Babo
in accordance with
their mother's
instruction   from   thorax
or from the   radio
waves   that controlled
her mind,   her thought
processes and processed her individual dialect
and dialectic statements
intended specifically
to instill private belief
of the megalomania
knowledge factors
she alone had
privy to   in her
babies   those children
she bore   and   who
were expected to
bear witness   to
her testimonies
her "Electronic computer
PUP-PET-RY!
Comb your
hair   children!"   informing
those surrounding her
and surrounded by   her
voice
apart from   the crowd

a part of   their lives
they walked two
aisles over from her
in the Piggly Wiggly
listening to her
through the aisles and
hearing the comments
from strangers
from   pass-her-bys
in shock,   in awe,
in obliviation   to
her informative
speeches   and   semi-
silenced whispersssss
breaking silence
absolute with "ssssss"
and vulgarities
"Get off my vulva.
You damn, dirty
pimps.   United States
government   prop-a-gan-da,"
she says and
grabs a box of
Kellogg's Corn Flakes   for
her husband.
"Quit raping me
with radio waves,"
she orders and
pushes the cart
with the broken
wheel skidding
slowly up the
row of   canned
goods and she
screams,   "Buggers,
PIMPS, IBM,

Esso, United States
Air Force,   you are
ALL   in this together!"
and they say
"listen to that woman,
who is she?"
as if they didn't
know   and she
whispers,   "Sssssso,
you think you have
fooled me with thisssss
plot, thissss ssssscheme
to rule my mind.
Not thissss TIME!"   Then
she wheels into the checkout and
exchanges pleasantries
with the checker
whom she calls
"Dear"   and gets upset
if she isn't addressed
by her last name
with formal prefix
the children try the
coin return   on all
vending   machines
within preschool   and
early elementary
grade reach of extremities
they run to the
Studebaker   as she
carries out   the
brown paper sacks
with nineteen-cent loaves of
bread and food for
five for a few
days   which in their

reality is supposed
to last them at least
a week or two,
and could very possibly as their
mother rants too
much to boil eggs
and they make the
cheese and macaroni
independently   by
three and try   when
they are younger toddlers
and due   to the
anorectic condition
of little sister   who
has the syndrome
at least a decade
before   the   word   is
coined for marketplace
they crawl over each
other   to the back
the very rear of
the wagon,   the middle
seat occupied by one
the oldest child
the other two in
the rear   and the
other three,   or four,
dead at birth or
shortly thereafter   as
the children have already
been informed by
their mother while
tucking them in at
night   when she thinks
it opportune   to
implant this knowledge

she alone walks with
she keys the ignition
rolling the engine past
sputters and knocks
the children appreciate
the pink, so pink, fin-tailed
Buick   next to them
and wish they had
a newer model like
that   it looks like
a spaceship to them
seven years before
the moon landing
where their mother
sometimes   resides now
applying foot to pedal
she squeals out   in
reverse   carts scattering
her path   and begins,
"Never, never, never,
before   here   were we
violated by these
computer puppets
these objects of technology!"
and the children fish
through sacks   for
animal crackers   they
threw into the cart
when she wasn't looking
knowing she wouldn't
know the difference
because she was "busy"
they pass by the
light   before   the train
crossing,   "Do you
see anything?"   the

lights flashing and boards, striped,
falling   in front of   the
grill,   "No, of course not,"
older sister says
and she proceeds
the train pouring on speed
as if there were no
time to s-l-o-w for
passenger cars
blowing its whistle
of Santa Fe and Atchison
Topeka and Ashland City
Tennessee   and they pass
the rear end tail pushed by
winds off of the rail in
time, in time, with the
beat of the rail
da-nan-da-nan-da-nan-da-nan
the heartbeat of railroad
suddenly the wooden
bar goes through the back
   CHKCHKCHKCHKCHK
   PINGGGGGGPINGGGGGG
windshield on the far
side   and the children gasp
for breath and eat more
cookies   looking carefully
for witnesses   they tell
her, "go on, no one saw"
and she complies   it
has begun to sleet
and the ice rain is
falling on the streets
on cars   and on the
car of children   and
their mother   or

imposter   of mother
they're not really
sure yet   and it
freezes   patches of
the front   windshield
and sleets   through the
back   little sister
imagines the ice accumulations
windows   to another   place
she traces   in her   mind
and sings   "jimmy crack corn"
and "mama may have"   to
herself   her brother hits
and pulls her hair   and
sister sticks out her
tongue   she smiles
and sings louder   her
mother turning the
lyrics around, "Jimmy
Crack Corn the Master,
the Master, the Master,
the president of the
United States and the president
of the AMA"   and they
go down iced streets
the tobacco road
they follow   the girl
turns to Indian lullabies
her dad sings her to
sleep with   and the
mother says, "Don't you
make fun of your father!
He has a beautiful voice!"
and she is only trying
to sound   like him
to get away   from her

and the mother says,
"Buckle your seatbelts
the buggers are going
to make me wreck."
and the older sister
takes off her seatbelt
and dives headfirst into the floorboard
insuring complete concussion
she is unconscious now
the baby boy is
strapped into a belt
by   little sister   and
she glances out
to see a blue blurrr
of a car   through   the
iced windshield   and her
mother's concentration
on hitting this car
head on   and   she grasps
the back of the middle
seat and hangs on for
life, her life,   though
she doesn't really want
it saved   and by seven years of age
will be slitting her
wrists   and surviving that
anyway   because she
has the survival skills
the urgency to maintain
through anything   the
adaptability   of children
of the chronically
insane   parental influence
she grabs and holds   hard
and her mother slowly,
carefully, deliberately

drives into the innocent
car   steering   slammmmming
into the car which
tears off the front fender,
driver's door, rear wheel and
breaks the glass
next to little sister's
cheeks   and careening off
the shoulder   trying
to steer away from
this mad woman
they assume   has lost
control of the wheel
when quite the opposite
is true   the control
is within   her, or the
voices she hears,   or the
place of their   origin
her mind
the mother is now
unconscious, liquid red eyes,
canyon gashed brow flowing   in   concussion
the older sister   is still   asleep
the baby is eating a
cookie   the other car's
passengers walking over
little sister pretends
to be knocked out
the police come
it is snowing   and a dark complexioned
man looks through
the broken rear windows
and sees the railroad
crossing bar
the little sister   waves to him
and he calls her

from the car
she sits in his police car
and calls her dad
on the two-way
"one adam twelve,
is this daddy?
one adam twelve,
calling daddy.
daddy are you in?"
the father asks
"Whose phone are you
on, who   dialed   for   you?"   "the copper's,
it's his"   and they   exchange
information of
insanity   of
split realities of
the mother   and
the children   the dad and the cop
little sister smiles
at all the people
gathering   and is proud
she could use a
police phone   and remember
the number   no one
ever taught her
she learned to memorize   by
teaching herself numbers and letters
she is three
she will always
remember this day
days   of   perspectives
that   other
people   will
never   be able   to
relate   to   without
an Artaud   in the

family   themselves
and when she grows
she will feed the
homeless   schizophrenics
she sees   wandering
streets   and   tobacco roads
and know that without her
father   her   mother
would have ended up
down the same path
of the pitiful   who
walk the other side
while they reside here
those that see   the   s p a c e
between second and third
dimensional arts   and speak it
the children witness
and play transistor radios

COLOPHON

Dog Road Woman was designed by
Becky Weinberg and Allan Kornblum, using
Adobe Caslon and Cochin typefaces. Coffee House books
are printed on acid-free paper, and are smyth sewn for
reading comfort and durability.